OLD-TIMERS

by Carol Talley
illustrated by Ron Mahoney

PEARSON

Scott
Foresman

Editorial Offices: Glenview, Illinois • Parsippany, New Jersey • New York, New York
Sales Offices: Needham, Massachusetts • Duluth, Georgia • Glenview, Illinois
Coppell, Texas • Ontario, California • Mesa, Arizona

Every effort has been made to secure permission and provide appropriate credit for photographic material. The publisher deeply regrets any omission and pledges to correct errors called to its attention in subsequent editions.

Unless otherwise acknowledged, all photographs are the property of Scott Foresman, a division of Pearson Education.

Photo locators denoted as follows: Top (T), Center (C), Bottom (B), Left (L), Right (R), Background (Bkgd)

Illustrations by Ron Mahoney

ISBN: 0-328-13595-X

2 3 4 5 6 7 8 9 10 V0G1 14 13 12 11 10 09 08 07 06 05

The town of Willow Creek, Missouri, has 398 people and five fire trucks. The volunteer firefighters lump all the fire trucks together and talk about their fire "apparatus," but they just mean their fire trucks. And some folks lump all the volunteer firefighters together as "fire*men*," but that's not right. There's Doris Bonner, who has been a volunteer for more than ten years.

Anyway, back to the fire trucks, or apparatus. You may be thinking that five fire trucks is a lot for such a small town, but the Willow Creek Volunteer Fire Department covers more than a hundred square miles of farmland and woods too. If there is a big fire over in Mack Springs or Howstis or North Plains, the Willow Creek crew helps out there. Like the sign at the fire station reads, "If we are called, we will go." Anyway, I was going to tell you about the fire trucks.

WILLOW CREEK
population
398

We have a ladder truck with a forty-foot ladder and a tanker truck that carries 2,500 gallons of water. There's also a pickup that is used to fight grass fires, a brand new pumper that can pump 1,250 gallons of water a minute, and another pumper that is more than a hundred years old. It hasn't put out a fire since before my grandpa was born. How that last piece of apparatus joined the Willow Creek lineup is what this story is all about.

It all started when they decided to tear down the old McKinley warehouse. The place hadn't been used in years. It was full of junk—wooden crates, worn-out car parts, and pieces of tin roof. Just rust and dust. Except, there was this one thing that looked interesting. Nobody was sure just what it was at first. It had wheels anyway.

Sure, it was red, but a faded, sorry sort of red. It looked like a circus wagon, or maybe one of those things they push around at the state fair, selling ice cream.

If you guessed that this was the old fire wagon, you're right. But it wasn't so easy to tell when Bobby Keller and I first found it. We were tinkering with some of the old junk in the warehouse one day. We didn't even see the thing at first. It was in the very back of the warehouse.

The tip-off came when Bobby noticed letters on the side. He said the letters looked like V.I.P. and maybe this wagon belonged to a Very Important Person. Then Mark Donovan came along and said they were V.F.D., which stands for Volunteer Fire Department. Mark ought to know. He's been a volunteer for twenty years. We knew we had some kind of fire apparatus, even if it didn't look like anything we had ever seen at the fire station.

Then Mark went and found Bud Thompson. Bud used to be the volunteer fire chief. He's been retired for a long time, though.

"Sorry," Bud said, "but even I don't go back as far as that old thing." He walked all around the wagon, looking inside and underneath.

Well, of course we weren't going to let them pull the warehouse down on top of it, whatever it was. So we hauled it down to the fire station, where we could stand and stare at it some more. After a while Bud had an idea. "You know," he said, "there's one person who might be able to tell us something about this thing."

"You mean there's somebody around here older than you?" joked Mark. Bud didn't say a thing. He just took a sip of his lemonade, unwrapped his sandwich from the Creekside Café, and took a bite. Mark finally gave in and asked, "Well, who is it? Aren't you going to tell us?" Bud took another drink of lemonade.

"Take State Road W until it forks at the cemetery. Follow the gravel road a mile or two and you'll come to the old Paterson place. I haven't seen him in a few years, but Ward Paterson must still be living out there." Bud paused to take a bite of his sandwich.

"He must be more than ninety. He used to be a good mechanic. He worked on the apparatus in the old days. He never was a firefighter, but his dad was the chief. Anyway, Ward Paterson is the one who might know something about this thing."

"Let's call him," said Mark. "Let's get him in here to look at it."

"Well, that could be a problem," said Bud. "I can't remember the last time Ward came to town. Apparently, he keeps to himself." And that's where they left it.

Two days later, I made up my mind to do something about the wagon. I took my camera down to the fire station, took half a dozen shots of the old red wagon, printed them off, got on my bike, and headed down State Road W.

It wasn't long before I saw an old farmhouse set back from the road. I had been pretty sure of myself up until then, but the sight of that house gave me the creeps.

Nobody lives there, I thought. It looked abandoned and lonely. I almost turned my bike around and headed back to town. But then I heard a motor running.

I turned my bike into the lane and headed up to the old house. I found Ward Paterson out in his barn, working on his tractor. With the sound of the motor going, he didn't even know I was there. I just let him work. He was old—older than my grandfather, even. But he was strong, and he looked like he knew what he was doing. When he walked around and shut off the engine, he finally noticed me standing in the doorway.

"Hello there," he said. "Who are you?" I told him my name, my dad's name, and my grandpa's name. "Well," he said, "I guess you go way back too."

Later, when Mr. Paterson and I were sitting on his front porch with my pictures, I could see the age in his face. But when he started telling me about the wagon, all of a sudden he looked a whole lot younger. He paced his yard as he talked.

"It's a pumper!" he told me. "Until this thing came along, all we had was the bucket brigade. This pumper was a big improvement, believe me! When the fire alarm sounded, this wagon was hauled right up to the fire. They dropped one set of hoses into the water. They used a well if there was one, but sometimes there was just a horse trough. They had to fill the pump with buckets of water. Then the men grabbed these wooden handles and pumped, up and down. Finally the water started flowing through the other set of fire hoses.

"It took eight or twelve strong men to keep a good stream of water going." Ward shook his head and laughed.

"Boy, I wish my daddy was here. He's the one who could really tell you about this old pumper. I wasn't even born when it came to Willow Creek. It was after the great fire, the one that almost burned down the whole town. After that disaster the Volunteer Fire Department got going and bought this pumper. My daddy told me about the day it was delivered on a railroad car. A crowd gathered at the station to watch the fire crew unload it. Of course, it wasn't brand new. The town couldn't afford that. But it was shiny red with bright brass trimmings. The men pulled her from the train station right down Main Street to the new fire station."

"Wait a minute, Ward!" (By this time he had told me to forget the "mister" stuff.) "What do you mean? The men pulled it? Didn't they have horses or mules or something to pull the thing?"

"On a lucky day, somebody might come along on a horse right when you needed one. But most of the time, it was pulled by manpower. One man grabbed onto the handle at the end and steered. The rest of them pulled on ropes fastened to the front axle, and off they went. I saw it myself when I was a boy." Ward picked up one of the pictures and looked at it for a long time. "Yeah," he said, "this thing is a real old-timer."

I suppose that could have been the end of the whole thing. The red wagon could have been shoved out behind the fire station or into some storage shed. It could have been left to rust away—along with its stories. Summer was almost over and it was time to think about going back to school. With one thing and another, I just didn't think about the pumper or Ward Paterson.

Then one day, right after the first day of school, I hit a rock in the road. My bike and I went skidding across the gravel and into a ditch.

I wasn't hurt, but my bike had a bad case of the wobbles. That's when I remembered Ward and all his tinkering.

Ward was glad to see me. He didn't offer me cocoa and cookies like old folks do in stories, but he was very happy to look at my bike. Before I knew it, he was taking things apart and clamping them to his workbench. I thought I could ride it home that very day, but Ward said he wanted to do some paint work. I ended up hiking out to Ward's every day that week after school.

The whole time I was watching Ward work on my bike, an idea was hatching in my head. Okay, I know. You're ahead of me, right? You're thinking that Ward could fix up that old pumper. Well, you're exactly right. I was getting a picture in my head—a motion picture—of that pumper, all shiny and new, rolling down Main Street with all the other Willow Creek fire apparatus in the big Fourth of July parade!

What did Ward think of my idea? Well, he was way ahead of me too. He had been thinking about that red wagon all this time. He wanted to see it the way it was when it first came to Willow Creek.

I'm not going to bore you with all the brilliant details of how I got the V.F.D. to subscribe to the restoration of this thing with their holiday party fund and their petty cash fund. Or how we had a fish fry and a pancake breakfast to raise more money to fix up the pumper. Or how Jerome T. Snyder III, the bank president, gave me his personal check to pay for the new paint sprayer and all the paint. By the first of January we had everything we needed, all gathered together in Ward's barn, including that rusty old red wagon.

I had a cold on the day they delivered the wagon out to Ward. You might say that's a flimsy excuse to miss the first day of restoration, but try convincing my mom!

It was a week later when I finally walked through the door of Ward's barn—along with my dad and Bobby Keller—and I almost had a relapse. The old pumper was lying all over the barn in a zillion pieces, like a big impossible jigsaw puzzle. How was the pumper supposed to survive this?

"There you are," said Ward. "I thought I was going to have to put this back together all by myself."

Two or three days a week after school and all day Saturday I would be out at Ward's barn working on the wagon. I learned why he had taken the pumper apart. That was the only way to get all the parts cleaned up. The iron parts, the wheels, and lots of odds and ends, had to be sanded down to the bare metal. Then we had to spray primer paint over everything and add three coats of red paint. All the brass and copper fixtures and trimmings had to be polished and varnished too.

By the time we got all those parts ready to put back together, my mom had planted her spring garden and we were on the last chapter of our history book in school. One day, I woke up and it was June—just a month left to get the wagon ready for the Fourth of July. I was really happy about how the wagon was looking.

With school out, all of us kids had time to spare, and we spent lots of days at the Paterson place. Sally Carter, the best artist at the high school, put the big V.F.D. letters back on the pumper and added gold pinstripes to the wheels. The Lewis twins built a wooden equipment box at the back of the wagon, like Ward remembered. Bud Thompson found some old canvas fire hoses in a shed behind the station and brought those out.

It seemed like everyone wanted to chip in. There wasn't a day that went by when someone wouldn't pop in to offer advice, or refreshments, or just to say hi.

Ward said there used to be a lantern that hung on the front of the wagon, but it was missing. We just figured the parade was in the daytime and nobody would notice. Then one day, we were sitting around watching paint dry. Bob Minskie, the fire chief over in North Plains came in carrying a genuine Volunteer Fire Department kerosene lantern. He said it was to thank the Willow Creek folks for all the times they helped out with brush fires in North Plains.

Some days, us kids just sat around and watched Ward work. We listened to his stories about the old days in Willow Creek. One day, he was tinkering with some brass parts on one of the rear wheels. I couldn't figure out what those parts could be.

"These pieces are called cams," said Ward. "It's kind of like when you fasten a playing card to the wheel of your bike and it makes a clicking sound when the wheel goes around. Well, these cams hit this brass gong with every turn of the wheel. It makes a terrific racket when the pumper gets going." I could tell we were about to hear another story.

"I remember the day the Sowder Hotel caught fire," Ward said. "It was on a Sunday. We were coming out of church and my mother said she smelled smoke. Then we saw it, billowing up over the trees.

"We all just stood there, except my daddy. He was already running when the fire bell started clanging. Daddy told me that in the early days they used to fire a .44 pistol for a fire alarm, but by this time they had a fire bell in the tower over the station. Anyway, he was off running, and we were all running after him.

"By the time we got to Main Street, he was already hauling on the ropes and pulling that pumper to the fire. These wheel cams here were striking the brass gong to beat the band.

"The hotel survived, but it was a close call. Lucky the flames didn't go above the second floor. The pumper wasn't much good any higher than that." Ward sat thinking a minute.

"I think maybe that was one of the last times the old pumper was used. The town was growing and needed something better. I think it was that same year the town got a Ford Model T fire truck. Then the hand pump wagon was retired."

"Well," I said, "it's coming out of retirement now!"

"That's right, boy!" Ward answered.

"And what about you, Ward?" I asked. "Are you coming along for the big parade?" He looked at me for a minute before he answered.

"Yes," he said. "I think I'll come along." He smiled to himself and started his tinkering again.

You've probably been to a bunch of parades on the Fourth of July, just like I have. But then, maybe you haven't, or maybe where you live they're different. So I'll tell you about ours. The marching band leads it off and plays the whole time—from the community center on First Street, all around the square, then back down Main Street to the Willow Creek Town Park. Behind comes every horse and rider for miles around. They are all dressed up and showing off their style. Then there's a bunch of guys in silly clown suits throwing prizes to all the kids. My dad is one of the clowns.

My favorite part of the parade is the fire trucks. The volunteer firefighters ride by on the ladder truck, the tanker, the pickup, and the new pumper, wearing all their gear, even if it's one hundred degrees in the shade.

This year, of course, there was something brand new, a blazing red and gold antique pumper fire wagon. They let eight of us kids, including me and Bobby Keller, haul the wagon by the new ropes on each side, and up front was Ward Paterson, steering us the whole way!

Helping Out in Your Community

When we think of citizenship, we may think first about being citizens of the United States of America. Being a good citizen of the United States includes respecting the laws of the country and the rights of other people. We are also citizens of our communities—our cities, towns, and neighborhoods. As citizens we can do a lot to keep our communities safe and fun. Most communities count on citizen volunteers to help do these things.

Volunteers help at art museums and perform in musical events. They work to preserve local heritage and historic buildings. They help keep parks and wildlife habitats beautiful. Volunteer firefighters and school crossing guards are examples of citizens who help keep other citizens safe.

A person is never too young or too old to be a volunteer. Everyone—from youngsters to old-timers—can help out!